SHAME IS
OCEAN
I SWIM
ACROSS

POEMS BY
MARY LAMBERT

NEW YORK

A Feiwel and Friends Book
An imprint of Macmillan Publishing Group, LLC
175 Fifth Avenue, New York, NY 10010

Lyrics from "Smoke Signals" by Phoebe Bridgers reprinted by permission of
Phoebe Bridgers and Marshall Vore, published by Whatever Music (ASCAP),
administered by Kobalt/Pizza Money Music (ASCAP).

Our books may be purchased in bulk for promotional, educational, or business
use. Please contact your local bookseller or the Macmillan Corporate and
Premium Sales Department at (800) 221-7945 ext. 5442 or by email at
MacmillanSpecialMarkets@macmillan.com.

Library of Congress Control Number: 2018936439

Book designed by Carol Ly
Feiwel and Friends logo designed by Filomena Tuosto
First edition, 2018

ISBN 9781250195890 (paperback)
10 9 8 7 6 5 4 3

ISBN 9781250195906 (hardcover)
10 9 8 7 6 5 4 3 2 1

ISBN 9781250211033 (signed edition)
10 9 8 7 6 5 4 3 2 1

fiercereads.com

CONTENTS

O N E
—

T W O
—

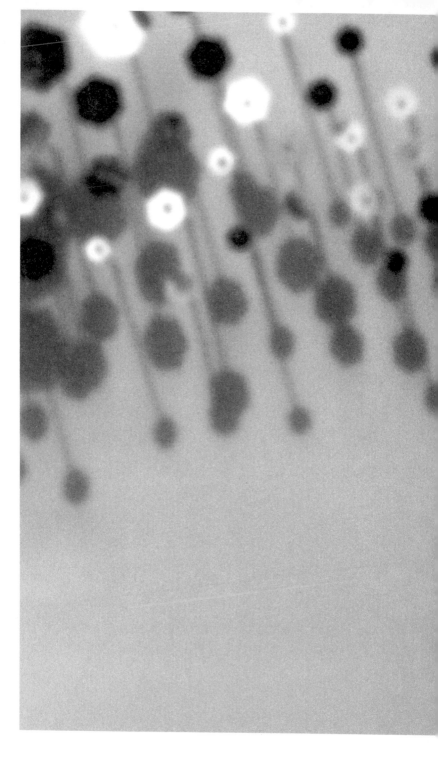

O N E

my body is terrifying,

idaho is a giant shithole,

and other wholesome stories

How I Learned to Love

When I was fifteen, I hated everything except for Weezer
and maybe like two people. And cereal.
One time a boy grabbed me in the music room
and kissed my neck in front of everybody.
I did not want to be kissed, but I thought I was supposed
to want to be kissed. I did not know what to do.
And so I laughed.
I knew you were supposed to laugh after things like that
The world had taught me to dress up my trauma
in short skirts and secret bathroom crying,
to protect the fragility of boys at all costs

When I was five, my father molested me
you become a strange human that way
You cannot whip yourself awake as a child
I should have been born a bird

When I turned six,
I stopped talking.

//

I am hurting so much this winter.
I am fucking everyone and nothing
matters, I wore braids to an award show, I started
wearing dark lipstick and crying in the shower

My sheets are beautiful, I kiss everyone I meet
The end of the world fits inside of my cocktail
I never fixed myself, I am my own arduous endeavor
I light myself on fire for everyone

I am the arsonist and the lover
All choked into one great sex bouquet
And Evelyn is here inside me, she is magnificent
and ordering room service like a pro

my mother still makes me cry from her love
& her sweet eyes & sugared compassion
the only parts I remember of my childhood
are lies I told myself to feel better

Epidemic

for Belltown

The girl with purple hair is sitting at my bar again.
I think she is beautiful.
But not in a way that I want to have awesome sex
with her but in a way that I want to drink chocolate
martinis together and go shopping for christmas vests
that have tinkly bells and even maybe polar bears
with hats on them.
She is having a full-body cry.
I am the worst bartender, simply because I don't know
how to counsel people without crying back at them.
She is crying about the state of women.
I know that we come from the same rotting wood,
so all I do is nod.

Rape is not a man behind a bush with a knife, she laughs,
It's kissing you on the mouth like whiskey at a nice bar.
The girl with purple hair and I are holding hands now
I only wanted an apology. An acknowledgement of
what occurred.

Grappling as artists, as girls, as ships in bottles,
how do we change any of it?

I tell her I am going to write a poem.

She says *no one wants to hear a rape poem*, mary

Rape Poem

Have you ever seen a stampede of horses?

Do you wonder what the hooves

look like from underneath?

Have you tasted the blood from biting

your own lips because you

couldn't say no loud enough?

I never fought back. I didn't punch him. I kept my

thighs tight and closed, but once he's inside you,

you wish you were a streetlamp.

    A seat belt.

    A box of nails, of rust, something hard and ruined.

You'll wish you were a wild pony, a slick fish on a line,

anything but a woman.

Once he's inside you, you just kind of give up

and your eyes glaze over.

They stay that way for years.

Tips for Fat Girls

you are the ugly best friend.

you are the misguided, the chubby comical relief,

you are the sweet girl with "inner beauty"

and you will always be second best.

the summer I turned nine, I gained fifty pounds.

it was the first time I ate an entire box of oreo cookies

the first time my reflection was foreign from weight

the first time I cradled my stomach like a child,

it was the first time I said, "mama. I hate my body.

I want to slice off these parts right here."

but I know better now.

I know girls like me have to grow a tough skin

always be ready for rejection

always be prepared to be left for the thin ones, yes

they will always leave you for the thin ones

be funny; laugh at yourself

you cannot afford to be quiet and sad

learn how to drink heavily

learn how to hide your vulnerability

become obsessed with your art

always turn the light off before fucking

always lay on your stomach

always be on a diet

always be generous

and when they take away the most beautiful,

sacred pieces of you that you have to offer, always smile

(you might at least have a cute face)

learn how to give head. be eager, be easy, be agreeable.

call the shit covering your bones something creative,

something like "curvy," or "a little extra"

stop calling them thunder thighs

(it only feels like earthquakes when you walk)

tell yourself that the aching will end,

that the tugging at your shirt

is because of the apron of your belly, hide it.

hide your roundness at all costs.

be molding clay.

be an anchor.

be dependable, be a model wearing heels.

yell at the scale, call her the devil's hooves

stop taking baths.

your body does not fit the way you want it to.

the water does not cover your awful.

throw up.

split yourself into two halves, call one half Your Mother.

tell her your diet is working, call the other half dove—no.

call the other half "shut up and smile"

call her Persephone, call her That Bitch

don't be a bitch! don't be a fat bitch, be nice,

be a work in progress, have an ego, be a Fierce Femme™!

wear makeup as if you can't stand to look at your own face

because femininity is the only thing they've left you with

you cannot afford to be without bronzer,

without teeth that sparkle,

hoopskirts, hair that curls, hair that "frames the face,"

get tattoos, quote marilyn monroe,

talk about renaissance painters,

never let them know how lonely it is

to have a body that is a joke,

the punch line in comedies, the "before" picture

never let them know you want to be something

other than the ugly best friend.

never let them know that the next person

to reach their hands into your chest

may look at you in awe,

at how surprisingly breakable you are,

how you have survived this long.

Why I Slept with Makeup on
for Five Years

for kelsey lauch, amanda redwood, and angela tislow

when i am sleeping,

i want to be a movie girl.

i want my hair to be cascading around my shoulders

lips still bright & eyelashes deep

want my monster to shine with a sephora glow

want you to see the pretty parts of me, even

angle my face to seem thinner in the dark

i am afraid

of my exposed naked, mostly my ugly—

this is my body

and i am terrified

of the things it can & cannot do

i wonder how many women

are painting themselves into movie girls

while they sleep

angling their faces alien

to themselves, an unnecessary surrender

to things that kill them,

to things that are not real

I tell myself in the mirror,

applying the second coat of mascara:

these things are not real

remind you that you are the god of your own beginning

if ever you falter or sink,
i will find a room of mirrors
it will be an endless room of gods, of you,
of choosing to live on purpose

I Will Fill a Tub with Iceberg Lettuce

if i told you about the bathtubs i wish i owned

just to kill myself artfully

you'd probably say hey,

this girl is fucking nuts.

maybe just two—one for utility, for the nightmare thing

and a second clawfoot to fill with iceberg lettuce—

not soggy, sad lettuce but crisp and happy,

glistening in the sheen of the light

after i've drowned myself, you can

put me on a bed of leaves

and it won't be figurative either!

like actually put me on top of the lettuce

like a christmas pig or roast beef

let the vultures come to me, i just—i mean to say,

gosh i still feel like dying these days

the meds are pretty good about

shutting up the choir of crazy

but when you have an obsession

with the glory of your own death

I Know Girls (Bodylove)

for anyone who has ever felt their body is incorrect

i know girls who are trying to fit into the social norm

like squeezing into last year's prom dress

i know girls who are low rise, mac eyeshadow,

and binge drinking

i know girls who wonder if they're disaster

and sexy enough to fit in

i know girls who are playing russian roulette

with death it's never easy to accept

that our bodies are fallible and flawed

but when do we draw the line? when the knife hits the skin?

because we're so obsessed with death—

some women just have more guts than others

the funny thing is women like us will never shoot.

we swallow pills,

still wanting to be beautiful at the morgue.

still proceeding to put on makeup

still hoping the mortician finds us fuckable

we might as well be buried with our shoes. and scarves.

and handbags.

we flirt with death every time we etch

a new tally-mark into our skin

i know how to split my wrists to reveal battlefields too,

but the time has come for us to reclaim our bodies.

Our bodies deserve more than to be

war-torn and collateral, offering this

fuckdom as a pathetic means to say:

i only know how to exist when i'm wanted

girls like us are hardly ever wanted, you know

we're used up. and sad. and drunk.

and perpetually waiting by the phone for someone to pick up

and say "you did good."

well, you did good.

try this:

take your hands over your bumpy lovebody naked

and remember the first time you touched someone

with the sole purpose of learning all of them,

touched them because the light was pretty on them

and the dust in the sunlight danced the way your heart did.

touch yourself with a purpose,

your body is the most beautiful royal

fathers and uncles are not claiming your knife anymore,

are not your razor, no—

you put the sharpness back.

lay your hands flat and feel the surface of scarred skin.

i once touched a tree with charred limbs

the stump was still breathing

but the tops were just ashy remains

i wonder what it's like to come back from that.

sometimes i feel forest fires

erupting from my wrists and the smoke signals sent out

are the most beautiful things i've ever seen

love your body the way your mother loved your baby feet

and brother, arm wrapping shoulders, remember,

this is important:

you are worth more than who you fuck,

you are worth more than a waistline,

you are worth more than beer bottles

displayed like drunken artifacts,

you are no less valuable as a size 16 than a size 4,

you are no less valuable as a 32A than a 36C

you are worth more than any naked body

could proclaim in the shadows,

you are worth more than your father's

mistake or a man's whim, your sexiness is defined by

concentric circles within your wood—wisdom & truth

you are a goddamn tree stump

with leaves sprouting out:

reborn.

My Weakness Is a Crooked Wheel
for C.R.U.

when i was little i used to cup my hands
over the flashlight
and watch my blood glow pink
i imagined the light piercing through my fingers
like an alien scanning me to another planet
the nice thing about disappearing
is you only think of the light

///

idaho is a goddamn piece of fuckity fucked shit.
you are living here, inside of the epicenter of shit
you are still pretty, still kind, wearing a vest
because you know i like to fuck women in vests.
so here you are in the chasm of an armpit
telling me that you hate it here too.

this is the steel door of reality,

watching you fail to grow up or make sense of your life,
too scared of your own greatness.
you left your job at party city in washington and then
got a job at a party city in boise, and i can't laugh
at you struggling to age in a comatose town—
in the seconds it takes to say your name
i am simultaneously asking for forgiveness.

I'm sorry I left you back there.
you deserve the home of my palms,
i can save you from this awful city,
love, i am all that i have ever been:
only for you, waiting for the light to
shock me out of my own body, you,
gravity on a lovely pair of legs. this
longing, this wrought history,
this quiet ending, a stupid town,
the small porch, we kissed through tears, my guilty
star, my stuttering tongue, my tenacity,
my old heart, the chemistry of the
language of glances, the way your unhappiness
is a small flood i cannot
sandbag into a song, the way that walking

toward you felt like rescue, the

way you want out of your own hurricane,

the way i am the boat, the way

i cannot swim either, the way we are both

folded into the riptide of this

odyssey

o, the weeping violins,

o, the anguish of memory

o, the beauty of the brush of hands—

I cannot leave you again.

i made myself a rose of clay around you, and now

i cannot fit the mold to a different cast,

love

my memory is a crooked wheel that perpetuates sadness

my memory is in love with you

i am trying to remember that these are just letters,

they do not talk.

a palm is a part of the hand.

i watch it light up.

i watch it disappear.

The Art of Shame

My mother found a rabid dog

And wanted to hug it

Wanted to give it all her glorious honeylove

Wanted to bathe her children in a two-parent household

But the dog didn't want kids.

The dog would scream it in the hallway at 4 a.m.

Oh the sheer art of it

how the monster could panic into my body;

sometimes I still hear it in my darkening sleep

the way some paintings haunt you

I am a museum,

I must be a museum

When I was seven

The dog told me I was going to be a slut

No one came over to our house to play

The dog made me write "I Will Flush the Bathroom Toilet"

seventy-five times. I would have remembered

to flush the toilet

but I started blacking out around then

forgetting basic things, praying that Oprah would save us all

I took snapshots with my memory camera, hoping

there would be justice for this kind of violence

that is more fear than breaking

no one knows what to name it

The teachers at the daycare offered apology eyes

and extra sequins for the art project the day

after the dog screamed me around each room

because I forgot where my other shoe was

When you are a child, and your mind is a fire alarm,

you lose the ability to remember simple things

I haven't lost a personal item in months.

Do not laugh when I say this is a victory.

Shame is an ocean I swim across

Sometimes I call it drowning

Sometimes I call it Moses

Sometimes I say Good Morning

and sway to its murky dirge

Sometimes I win and cut off its crest with a pink machete

Sometimes I want to fuck it and marry it

and kill it all at the same time

Sometimes I spend my whole day

apologizing on shame's behalf

Sometimes I think it must be an art form to feel this bad

Sometimes I outrun all of its psycho history

Other times I repeat the language from my child mouth

while beating my head against the wall

All the time, I am forgiven.

Jesus Loves My Crop Top

"These women need to stop glorifying unhealthy obesity"

—some dickhead

1 like my belly button.

2 My belly button does
not interrupt your life.

3 Why do you hate so
much my belly button?

4 Is it maybe because
someone was mean to
your belly button?

5 I'm sorry someone
was mean to your
perfect belly.

6 You cannot love what you
hope your body turns into
without loving it for what
it is, right now.

7 When I was in high school,
I obsessively fantasized about
taking a knife to my stomach
like a bagel slicer.

8 One night I found a website
that just had photos of girls
with stomach rolls and back
rolls and they were smiling
and I cried because I was
uncomfortable and envious
of their joy.

9 I used to drink a fifth of tequila
and smoke a pack of cigarettes
every night.

10 No one criticized my health then.

11 My body is what it is what it is.

12 The mirror is what it is what it is.

13 Celebrating your body is a
revolutionary act.

14 I feel my own self breathe.
I feel my organs when I breathe
and when I shower, I feel my
skin on my skin. I know that it
is mine. I listen to what my body
asks for. I put on a shirt that shows
my stomach. I wing my eyeliner
up and I ride my bike into the
sunset and I will pick wildflowers
with my love and later I will eat
brussels sprouts and maybe a
martini with lots of olives in
it and I will do all this because
it makes me feel good and because

I am worthy of love and cute
clothes and happiness.

15 Feeling worthy has taken a very
long time.

16 I am my own holy revolution,
welcome to the church of my
thunder thighs, I am awake
and alive, I've come to wear
all of the crop tops that the
glittering world has to offer,
I've come to dance the shame
out of my childhood, I've
come to win back my joy.
You may not snatch it from
me like a purse.

17 I win whether I have a mouth
full of pretzels or a mouth
full of kale; you have not
been granted the privilege
to know how I consume
my world and what makes
me most delight in my skin.
I will glorify the shit out of
my body.

I Was Thinking About You Today

When I loved my first real thing, I fell into her like Winter.

I call this love my "first love." With sugared nostalgia,

I murmur "first love" to my college friends,

to my bandmates, to the neighbor's dog.

It is no secret that I had emptied the truth of myself

to many before her. I suffocated doubt

with two hands, collapsed the neon parachute

of my ambition, fit all my lovers inside.

No questions.

I heard they liked women who drank whiskey

so I became the best at it.

I heard they liked women who thought themselves ugly

so I slammed my fists into my stomach

in the dim of a bathroom light.

I begged God for erasure, for newness, for thin,

for a body that shuts up.

I dyed my hair and then I dyed it back.

I shaved my armpits, and then I

grew them out. I wrote miles of music,

I found God all before my "first love."

I am older now and some of these things
have become me. I have had twenty incarnations.
I have taken some of the things I liked—
meditation or asking cashiers about their day—and
I have discarded others.
Just because I evolved, doesn't mean I am spineless.
Just because I am malleable, doesn't mean I am undeserving.

I will not apologize for being the shape of light & when.
What a blessing it was to be hugged gently
in a church. What a blessing it was to hear Rosie
Thomas in Rachael's truck. What a blessing to witness
true love, a wedding in a hospital courtyard,
what a blessing to be loved by the boy
who understood I could not kiss him the way
he wanted to be kissed, and let me go.
Love is a mirror, a map, a lesson in unfixed gifts.

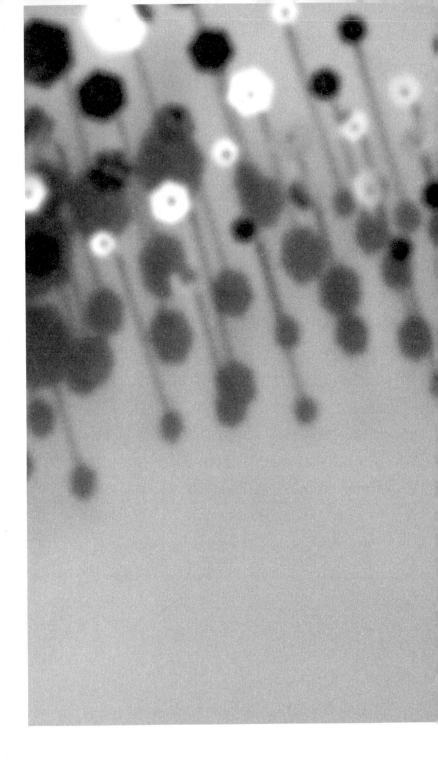

T W O

the good things are still flawed

and

i think i got intestinal problems because

farting is really hard to do when

you're in bed with a hot person

Valentine's Day

"relationships are just little cults" —Sam Sax

every day i want to write a new poem to you

because my heart is SO LOUD. so loud, all the time.

my heart is a pack of puppies

wagging their tails at each other

my heart is a camp counselor—first day

my heart is a boat, full of smiling people

in bright shirts dancing the cha-cha

my heart is beach day. no shoes.

i mean to say you make me feel like

the sun isn't trying to kill me

you make me feel like someone just paid for my groceries

the flowers you bought me two weeks ago

are still yellow and bursting

I forgot to tell you

my heart is still yellow and bursting too

sometimes after we kiss I want to crawl

underneath the floorboards

and giggle to myself

i think: "this person keeps kissing me on purpose!"

i also think: love is a delicious weapon

i keep hurtling myself into the sky & sand of it

when you are gone, i sleep with your

hologram in a pillow dream

and i say goodnight from the aquarium of heavy eyes

smiling lazily ear to ear

I can't believe I'm the one you tell your good news to.

Saturday Night Extravagance

It is Saturday night in Belltown.

The bars are thumping of techno and bad decisions,

the sidewalks alight like schools of fish,

bodies painted in short silver skirts, glitter and

axe body spray. The straight people are out

tonight and they are very shiny! When we enter

our apartment, the sidewalk sounds like a

nightclub submarine, an overhead speaker of

warbled bros hitting on woo girls and something

about Stephanie needing her bitches and hating her shoes.

You and I have spent the day at IKEA,

because while eating dinner on the

floor is very "primitive-chic" of us,

it is uncomfortable for my modern

ass. After assembling our dining room table

and chairs for three hours we are

quietly sitting in bed. I am picking out more

furniture I want to buy online, saying

each product name out loud and giggling, "IVANSKA
BLENKAR! WHAT DOES IT MEAN!" You are
beside me, sorting through the mail in an oversized
T-shirt, now razor-focused on clipping
coupons from the Valpak.

Simultaneously we look at each other, as if we'd had
the same sad thought. This is our Saturday Night.
This is our extravagance. I am twenty-three!
The question pooled around in my head, making
circles within itself: "Is it okay that this makes
me happy? Is it okay that I am content in this normalcy?"
You smile at me in a white shirt with hot sauce stains.

Yes. With all that my foolish, domestic heart
possesses, I love this. Our little apartment
with all of its stories of brick and doors to nowhere, I
love that you hold my hand before you fall asleep,
that you love to cook me every meal, I love
that my heart is a window I didn't know was open,
I love your frugality, that you clip coupons to get
The Best Deal, and you're remorseful when you don't,
I love that our fights are fair and infrequent,

I love the way my mouth says your name, like music

crawling out of a cave, I love that when we kiss it is

the champion of all other things that lips can do

or have done since: the bells that ring and the snow that

sits and the city of my

talking hushed from the

simple sealing of my quiet mouth resting on yours.

This Saturday night, every Saturday night,

far surpasses any distilled grain, any

pair of fishnet stockings, any diamond parade.

Yes, I want the promise of the cathedral

of your mouth for the rest of my life.

Yes, I want to be the temple of your unraveling.

Yes, I want to be your chosen partner in the

IKEA shit-show supermall

where couples go to die.

What an extravagant love.

Portrait of the Lover as a Dalí Painting

On the phone I hear myself say

"I'll take what I can get from you"

and I feel stupid, like I'm one of those

romantics forever pasted in a

Salvador Dalí painting, yes, there, that's me

My body, a boat's sails, the boat's sails are butterflies

That's me again, just a casual wild

elephant with a tuba for a head

Yes, I love you, also my love is kind of like a clock

melting in a desert

I mean to say that when I met you,

time felt like it bent itself

I forgot what proportion was

because I felt infinite and forever changed.

As you turn to leave me for the last time

in front of my gate,

I purse my lips to form the word "bitch"

instead all I can think to say is Please.

Please don't go.

Please let your fingers itch

for the phone a little longer

and don't stop yourself this time,

please don't let your legs slide

under mine when you're sleeping

unless you mean it, please mean it

please show me the woman you are

when you are honest, when you are weak

please hold my body like touching

the dog-eared pages of a book

like I am precious and well-loved. Wait!

I can be better!

I can be skinnier! I can be funnier!

I can care less, wait!

let me try undressing without my back turned,

I can papercrane myself into a mold,

any mold, what would you like me to be

please be careful with my folding wings

please have more to say than sarcasm, say rose

floating in the desert, tell the truth,

say you're scared of me

I Am Asking You to Be a Crowbar

When your hands rested upon me,
it was like someone brushing cobwebs
from a family heirloom. My body, a silver
candlestick. A painting of geese on the lake.
Your eyes glowing like a welder's torch.
I forgot what lungs do, could you tell?

At the restaurant, the electric nausea
of new love ping-pongs in my organs.
Beats of wings stretching the length
of my torso rattle against the table.
Pay no attention to the bird.
What were you saying
about dancing?

I imagine you taking your smash
to me with a steel wrecking bar.
I imagine all the blood and sinew and truth,
veins dangling like phone wires,
spilling over the café table.

I imagine exhaling, finally.

Neither of us flinching.

I bet it is peaceful to watch a bird

break restaurant glass. I smile demurely.

Our dinner resumes. How is your sister?

I readjust my dress.

You look so beautiful tonight.

Kaitlin, the Choreographer

i've always wanted my limbs to swing that way

so musical and concise, salsa

hipswivel bent, fast and sweat, sexy.

i can see you scanning me with your eyes,

when we talk it's dumb how reckless i feel,

so small, so nervous, i know you know

what it means to love something magically unhuman

like music or dance or the fluidity of sound and body

when you look at the mirror

and see bones as bridges

muscle as a language

as a catalyst do you ever ask yourself

if you could love anyone the way you love

watching bodies in motion,

moving the way you want them to.

i don't know if you could.

my bet's on the mirror.

8

There was a gay couple I met last year that was
celebrating their eighth wedding to each other,
this time in Washington.
With each state that
passed a gay marriage vote, they would travel and
get a document of marriage in that particular state.
Part of me thinks that is ridiculous and excessive
most of me thinks that it is wildly romantic
but I'm telling you:
once I held your face in my hands,
pressed to my mouth, aching of forever
I understood
I would marry you eight times, too.

The Airport Is Switzerland

I have been gone for six weeks this time.
We have a day and a half to be together
before I leave again for the road;
I don't know if I can bear it

Our time is always a pendulum
Is always sporadic and sparse
I cannot seem to collect myself
at the loading zone of the Bradley airport
This place is Switzerland
Is both friend and ache
She hangs us, suspended in midair
Until the next time I see you
under the covered concrete for the
Welcome Home
How extraordinary it is to feel your own heart gasp
Welcome home to my arms,
to my hungry eyes, to my full anatomy

And in the inverse; the leaving

My cells bend involuntarily when it is

the kiss of departing

I pull for you physiologically like a tide

Our never-goodbyes (only see-you-soons)

Circle like full moons

but I still tremble with the friction

that comes before the silence

I do my best to remember the idea

of great joy and great sorrow

And that you cannot have one without the other

The airport is a lesson in two worlds

The flight is a test of each

When I go,

I can't help but feel the continental United States

is a tidal wave ripping us far apart

I blame this on geography and the ocean and the moons

All of me wants to rebel in this instant

Say "fuck it. I'm gonna chop wood and

make banana bread and kiss you for the rest of my life"

I choose you

You said to me, crying last night

I choose you back

I hope you know every day

I choose you I choose you I choose you

I choose the ache and the waves of hot tears,

and the fast plane and the windows of time,

the brilliant hours of magic

in a field by your house, the two worlds,

the anatomy of your cells, the holy welcome

of your arms, the tears of our curbside goodbyes

oh my truest love—

It is a privilege to miss you.

My Friends and I Were in a
Ninety-Mile-an-Hour Collision

and we should have died. it's real what they say,
everything flies around you in slow motion, lights
blinding, sound as an aftermath, and is that my voice
screaming or hers. all i felt was the shooting pain up
and down my leg, she stayed with me sitting in the
passenger's side and doesn't remember. I cried like I
was reborn with blood on my hair, i thought i lost her
then, i never lost her and now i cant forget her, she
sat on the curb as i tried to make bad jokes we found
out she had a concussion but truly i don't know how
to explain that when the car hit us i thought i was
the crumpled metal too that i was the weight of the
engine on our bodies, was the torture of high school
all compiled into one really loud scream, i didn't even
know my voice made sounds like that

Written at Our Dining Room Table

I stared at the back of Henry Seedorf's head
for all of sixth grade.
One time he was singing a "Weird Al" Yankovic
song about Star Wars during free time and I knew the
harmony so I sang along.
I knew the back of his head way better than the front.
He had a mole on the left side of his neck
I studied it every day to make sure it wasn't cancerous
That was my favorite part of sixth grade.
Tonight over dinner, I think about the back of your head
and make a note that I ought to study it
It is important to know one's partner's
back of the head for many reasons.
Maybe one day we'll be on a famous lesbian couples
game show, and I'll need to point out your glorious
cranium out of ten less attractive heads
I mean, I know the front of your head really well
You have my favorite head
But I want to adore all parts of you equally

I feel a twinge of guilt that perhaps I have not given the
proper attention to the back of your head

I think about the day we met and how you made dinner
I remember watching you move like a symphony
conductor, swiveling around the linoleum,
talking passionately with your hands
as I stood idle with a jar of water,
smitten by your skill and the conversation.
I pretended I was your girlfriend and we lived like this
with you gliding around the kitchen and how maybe
you'd kiss me in between chopping vegetables.
I imagined staring across from you at our dining room
table thinking about how I could best love you.

Your New Girlfriend Is Pretty
and I Hate Her

when you say good morning from your flannel sheets

and the night is still thick from your fucking in this room

i imagine a halo around your skin

seeing it like i used to.

the undertaker, with soft doe eyes,

says "good morning" back to you

at least that's how i imagine it in my head when

you say good morning to another woman

she must be my killer

she must be my evil end

when she opens her mouth,

does she know how we spent the year?

drunkenly, buckling

under the truth of being stupid and nineteen

how i didn't know you bought me a ring

how you placed it on the dresser when you left

does my heartbreak echo in the hall

of your mouth after you kiss?

—

unless?

unless the undertaker has really pretty hair

and you love her

then it's not really that bad.

maybe she's not an undertaker after all.

maybe she's just like a perfect face but maybe

when she holds your hand does it feel

like the strings of the piano might snap

the weight of the attic might collapse

are there boxes of my letters underneath your old clothes

are they chorusing an album that i don't dare play

(endless numbered days) i know you know you are

always in parentheses for me

oh my lost love

there is no undertaker

there is no evil laugh

i'm just writing a poem about you

and your beautiful new girl

and trying to not get coiled into a dream

that is hard to forget

a memory tough to shake, little scars

i should have known that something so honest

couldn't last the greed of my mouth

You Are with the Wrong Person

It was a joke, mary

You are so young and drunk and sensitive

Your eyes dart back and forth like fish in a pet store

waiting for approval

I'm going to teach you to toughen up, kid

And I know a lot about being cool,

And then she would glide across the floor

and make smart jokes

and I would clap my uncool hands

So proud

Most of my life I've felt like

a shopping cart with a shitty wheel

Been too weirdo

too chubby girl

too excited

All I wanted was to convince her

that I was useful and smart

and not even magazine-cool, just regular-cool

I'm not saying that she didn't love me good enough

I'm not saying she didn't hold me with tenderness

in the hours of falling asleep;

That after torrential rain bent our frames into making—

we did grow to love each other

But there is something that happens

when you are told you are Too Much

You begin to ask everyone,

how small would you like me?

What I Thought About While We
Fell Asleep Watching *Chopped*
for MB

I want to fold myself into a word written on paper
safe safe safe, tuck it inside of every lapel
i carry your love like a candleless flame

through the rooms of my house in the palm of my
hand. ok, yes: this could be a lightning miracle dive
that burns too fast. a darling sparkling in the hall.

a kamikaze of light & hurt & impulse. but here's my
confidence: I've got flint, faith, a penchant for good
endings. two strong hands. let's both of us sit in the

glow for a little while. discover the untethering, the
miracle of open windows, my heart wide as a bell for
you, chiming all through brooklyn. and if perhaps

you like the open windows and would rather leave,
I will still smile my joy at every burning coastline

knowing that while we drove to dinner or walked the

dog, or slow danced in the kitchen at the farm, I felt
like a million bucks just thumbing the hem of your
collar, a thief, a spark

Language Barrier

I read that in Japanese there is a word

for the light that passes through the trees

I wish I had a word for the way you look at me

I could say your eyes are the sound

of wooden chimes in winter

or the dust of the thicket awakening from sunbeams

when the snow clears

I want to say something, some accurate alchemy,

Some kind of splendor

to mirror in syntax

the kind of ceremony in your eye patterns

when you study my face in bed,

like I am being understood from the ground up

What kind of magic are you

The Last Time It Was Good

Your friends got married on a campground
in southern Washington.
Everyone was invited to stay overnight in bunk bed cabins;
it felt like a cool kids' summer camp
I was too poor to ever go to.

The wedding was beautiful.
The tables had perfectly homemade centerpieces,
the flowers—fresh from the market and placed playfully
in mason jars, bluegrass music
floating in and out of the barn.
The bride and groom took a rowboat on the lake that said
"Just Married" on the back. It was so
tender and wholesome. I felt privileged to go.

So naturally, I got shit-faced and wore
a nurse hat all night
I laughed obnoxiously and asked multiple times
if there was a surgeon in the room
so I could have a "heart-to-heart" with someone.

I think my boob came out at some point

while I was jump dancing.

Within the hour, I was crying rivers

about my childhood

You know,

A typical saturday

I woke up, cotton-mouthed and hollow

my head pounding from the first light of morning,

piercing through the cabin windows at 5 a.m.

I squinted my eyes as I opened the cabin door

Ready to make the trek to the main house for some water.

You stirred by the noise of the door, likely exhausted

by assuaging the blow of my alcohol-induced trauma parade

We had been fighting a lot around that time, always

coming to the conclusion that maybe we were too different

I was too soft, and you were too cool and the

glow of two years had long become pale, but

We will fight this! and Love will prevail!

We loved each other like an ongoing apology.

I was the only one awake when I stepped
onto the grass in my socks
My breath involuntarily pulled itself back into my body.
I had walked into a photo of a lake, quiet and dreamlike
The fog of the morning wrapped
around the edges of the water
Like a Bob Ross painting or a movie with Rachel McAdams
My mouth fell onto my kneecaps and I swiveled
around like a child in my socks and hopped
onto the mattress. Hangover be damned,
this was too beautiful to be selfishly observed.

You mirrored my enthusiasm for the glow
and the fog and the dream, suggested we
take one of the green camp rowboats out onto the lake.
I remember that morning vividly
my eyes crusted from crying
Staring across from you
your cheeks smudged with campfire ash.
We smiled weakly at each other,
and I told myself we were good.
I promised I would stop drinking so much.
You believed me.

I looked over the boat at my reflection in the water.

I looked kind of happy

for someone who was drowning.

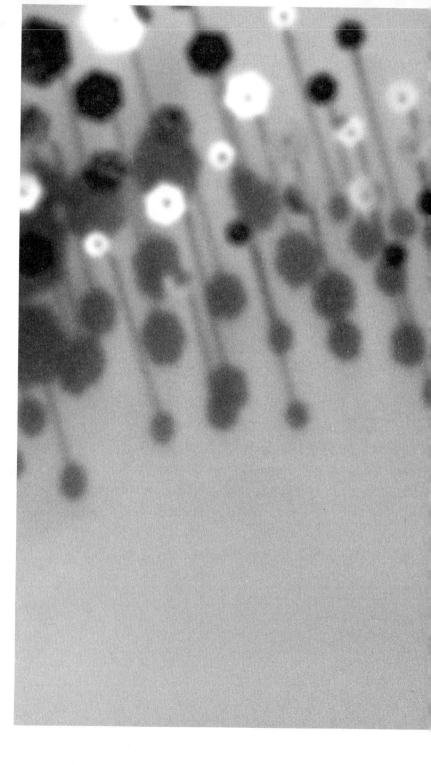

T H R E E

Congratulations, you are bipolar

Explanation of How Things Work

My heart, a mansion
Too many rooms
Not enough warm
shuttered big and blue

My heart a mansion
Too many rooms
Crawled into myself
Burned the roof

My father, kite string
Tied taut across yard
Encircled around my neck
Now I never forget

I never forget

Grief Is a Sundress and I Am Starving

You stood in the kitchen doorway just before bed. I
rested my body in a gentle lean against your back,
after a year of crying. The sand of last Summer. Like
a ghost without a bedroom, finding a wall. I wanted to
tell you that I tried my best to get up from the indent
in the couch where I spent October. And the parties.
And Christmas, my love, but I just couldn't. I couldn't,
and I wanted to and I want you to know that. My body
is a crater   in the living room, and you are a perfect
moon, and I am going to ruin you. Imagine your heart
as a Hitchcock movie, ok? Imagine a shower curtain.
My brain is a lurking shadow. Crooked, sometimes
not there. When I was six and they asked me what I
wanted to be when I grew up, my eyes got big and I
said: SPACE. There is no more room in my head. I
wanted to write something redemptive tonight, but the
shame is so loud, it has become thick in my eardrum, I
could paint the room with it. Gigantic. *I buried a hatchet
/ it's coming up lavender / the future is unwritten / the
past is a corridor* I'm at the exit, she sings. Will my brain

hum itself into not eating again? Will I monster myself
in the dark? I can spin for days, it's actually quite
amazing. Seventy-two hours, I'm talking. No sleep, no
appetite. Forced spinach & threw it up. Did you want
to know these things? Is this helpful?

+

Ok, fine, I'll try something different. If it doesn't
work, I'll go back to being a black hole. The safety
of throwing yourself into a window. Ok, here we
go. Like jumping off a cliff into the river: I have nice
fingernails? I'm trying to take care of myself? I drink
less now? this feels terrible. Like eating celery. Lucille
Clifton says: Say it clear and it will be beautiful. OK,
Lucille. I had a manic episode that lasted for months. I
was not on a boat in Spain eating tapas at the end of it, I
was exhausted. An ocean of concrete and sitting in my
own shit. I don't know if that is beautiful. I don't know
what it is like to love me. Probably like having knives
for hands and wanting to itch your back. Or caring for
a lion that doesn't know it is dying and is also going
to kill you on accident. I have never been soft & slow

like a moonrise. But I guess this is the part where I say "it's a process." That is a smart thing to say. Pragmatic. I am doing my best and you are a patient song. The one that sings about Walden and burning trash on the beach. My brain might trick me into my speed brain again, maybe next summer or some unsuspecting weekend in LA, but I am a person that exists, and I took a shower today. And maybe tomorrow I will eat a full meal. There is always a thing or a dad that says "you are a piece of shit," boring their own hell into my head, and yes, the brain is a disappointing masterpiece, but hopefully I get better each time and learn how to stuff socks in the mouths of monsters. Hopefully there is enough chocolate and TV marathoning and crying and unlearning to get through life, and every time it gets just a little bit easier.

Hey, look at that. Something redemptive.

If Bodies Are Speaking Vessels for God, Then This Is a Poetic Conversation We Had While You Raped Me

I am a country with hands and you
are a thing with a mouth. mandy,
was it? sorry my body is a burning
home, everyone wants out or they
want a redeeming story about the
arsonist, they want to hear the
interesting parts about Iraq, not the
slow pain, only the camaraderie, but
my friends are dead and your hair is
soft. When I was young and sad and
hungry I learned how to guillotine a
tulip like you with my eyes closed.
why do you look like that, angel?
you asked for this headlessness—
your neck, a white flower waiting for
teeth. Face all wide like a teenage
girl or a deer I shot once that didn't
die right away—Look at me, canyon

eyes, whats-her-name, Look at this
drunken palace you've brought me.
Look at the world I do not have,
how it does not open to me, how
your thighs are closed like a golden
challenge I have always deserved,
how your June July Calendar hips
sang to me in the hall, asked me to
choke them into a waltz. I'm here
alone and I need a friend, an arrow,
an animal to kill. for fucks sake
look alive

Chris, my name is God.
You will not remember these
moments, these death maneuvers,
these horror orchids. How the shape
of your violentmouth turned into a
kiln born inside children that I do
not have yet—Watch when you turn
my please don't into a knotted snake
around my neck, watch how your
teeth puncture my Every Morning,
the residual memorial of my body.
My please don't sits cross-legged in
an underwater arcade, slurred—but
Chris, know that they hear this
please don't in infinite heavens.
Could you bring me another year? a
different body in the shape of a
red tulip field—Oh, God. This is the
part where I laugh because I can't
scream to shatter your bed, cannot kill my
father, cannot denounce the gift of
living or break you Chris: I can only
laugh high-pitched and maniacally,

curdle inside of the coffin of my
mind, can only survive. I will
remember you for the rest of my
life. how everything is glowing
white. You will not think of me, will
give me a different name and story
and I will wear it around my neck
like a diamond noose. When I put
on my jeans quietly in the morning,
Chris, don't
mention an animal you killed when
you were just a boy. Don't
say that it didn't die right away.

Depression Is Finding a Peanut Under Your Boob in the Shower, When You Don't Remember Eating Peanuts

A hundred times I have laid in this spot
for an hour too long. Like a dead dog or an arsonist

the morning after a good burn,
still and charcoaled in a warm bed

It scares me, this thing of overstaying—
the pirated comfort in the hazard of What Happens If

What Happens If I never swallow food
again, if my collarbones collapse. If I lay here

until the moon circles again and I just pretend I'm dying.
What Happens If I run out of medication

or evaporate into the carpet or my head flies backward
I tell my therapist things like this, things like

⸺

I've never been so great at living,

I just repeatedly succeed at opening my eyes

after nightmares, somehow fumble into waking,

do not leave the house, somehow feed the cat

I say, *no one knows how many mountains there are*

in the world, do they? She says, *I'm glad you're here.*

On the Way to Therapy

I am at the intersection of 116

when something completely unexpected happens:

The town next to ours is having a parade today.

I am the last car allowed to pass on the parade route

before they close the street down.

My Subaru is the most special car on earth for five minutes.

the sidewalks are packed, lined with happy children,

waving at me like I am the town princess,

like I am here on purpose

the grandparents are watching the

happy children in plaid lawn chairs

there are balloons and american flags

and joy, trail mix and freeze tag

the air is all fresh grass and dogs and friendly neighbors

talking about their kids

some people start clapping for the show to start

the marching band is playing in the distance behind me

I smile real wide and wave proudly

as if I have done something worth cheering for

Brain Conditioning

All people are complex

All people want to be loved

However, I've found

that simple people are a gaggle of unicorns

Who have cut their complexities in half

They still exist as their whole selves

Just maimed in sad ways

from other assholes or dads who said

You can't be a flower

Or

Your mother was an idiot and so are you—

But maybe two simple people

who have lopped off their arms

finally feel understood

when they catch eyes across the bar

What is the loveliest form of being

and can I be that

I Washed Your Hair in the Sink

A swarm of dragonflies break themselves onto my windshield.
I, too, was in a car accident. The sky is a melon and
I am a brick at high velocity. I am a murderer. Then,
more bugs, their full wings, Jackson Pollocked on
the glass. This is where I start crying, "No! Please!
I'm sorry!" I say I'm sorry at least twenty times while
crying softly and I mean it. I really do. I want to drive
slowly, but I have to exist in this world and the other
cars behind me will be upset. My therapist says that
I need to work on balancing expectations, so I keep
driving fast and continue to cry. I'm a nice girl. I used
to be a dancer. Just when I feel calm, a family of five
geese splayed across the highway. I remember most the
feathers: dreamlike in the air, hundreds of punctured
pillows, crimson feathers dancing in slow motion. This
is when I pull over. I say enough.

*

In my dreams I kill my friends. These real awful,
grotesque movie murders. I don't want to be this
person. Scraped Scott's stomach with a melon baller.

I don't want to kill the bugs. The family of geese are honking, burned red into my mind. I'm a nice girl. It's getting moon outside. I wish I could stop. What a terrorlife, what a fluke.

*

I dreamt I stabbed you, love. I dreamt I pushed you in a lake by our old house. I'm sorry, I'm sorry. I don't know where this lives in me. Did I kill the geese? Did your heart die when I left our red room? Am I henchman or pallbearer? Am I breaking too? I'm sorry I was so selfish, so reckless. I used to twirl and have a musical laugh. I dreamt I was mud, had to hide your body in the dumpster. Had to bury you quickly, was not remorseful. How many times have you died now? The sky's electric pink, I can't stop crying. Just once I wish I would kill myself in my dreams, but I never do. Maybe I'm a coward. I miss dancing. Ninety miles an hour. The impact. You loved dragonflies. Tina's body. Brittany's ribs. Your face breaking the window. I washed your hair in the sink. I used to be a dancer. I am always a brick of feathers in my own throat, apologizing to you for the things I have done, plumes of white floating out of my mouth.

Grown

It is Summer. I am six. I accidentally swallowed
watermelon seeds in our backyard. I am sweating
in my shame. I am sure that I am pregnant.
The tree in the yard says "how pretty, how pink"
I hate pink. I hate my dad. I hate pink.
We don't have a yard. I didn't even eat watermelon.
I am on the playground, repeating the phrase
"just be a kid, learn how to be a kid"
Everyone I know is fascinated with the Earth.
But I don't care if the rain makes itself again
Recess is meant for chasing possible bachelors
to evaluate whether they could be good fathers.
I am in the foreground of the backyard that we do not have
I am pulling grass from my front teeth.
When I say grass I mean I didn't want to be kissed like that.
The garden was choking me.
Someone cut holes in my flower dress.
I am an incomplete.
ete/ete/ete
Incest is a skipping stone

Cutting me with a memory knife before bed

I am a child falling off of a bar stool

I don't have a backyard. The garden is choking me.

Stop it. There is no garden, Mary.

I am drinking too much.

I am throwing up. I am throwing up my

Hands, I do

I do want to know how clouds are made, I like

pink and I want a yard

I tattoo flowers on my arm and I missed it all

Jesus

I missed everything.

The Good News Is You Won the Lottery, the Bad News Is the Lottery Is Post-Traumatic Stress Disorder

what if I told you trauma was a stalker

follows me room to room

visits

me at work, leaves

dead animals on my day planner

texts me knives, licks

my memory before I have a chance to get it right

I am on all fours digging into the carpet

learning how to make wool imprints in my kneecaps

this is how I learned to dance

with half of my body on fire

there is not enough whiskey in the world

to make any of this bearable

but i have been digging in the basement

of my trauma

trying to find a window a light

a string a sound

something that doesn't read helpless

something that doesn't read sad girl crying all the time

a wreck in a shower

a wet mess huddled in a bed

don't look at me like that

like i can do better

like this sadness is a well that I jumped into on purpose

nothing is on purpose

my mania is so stupid and marvelous

it sits in a glass jar

teetering on the kitchen counter

I am always one slipped rug away from losing everything

Before

the farmer grew tomatoes and they were beautiful

they grew in the sweat of summer

the farmer loved the dirt

and she watered the plants well

the bees happily flitted around like

kids at a birthday party before social insecurity

and everyone was grateful for the rain

how it coaxed the burns of the sun

And when the farmer harvested tomatoes,

it was a red parade

she sold them in the market

and the people loved them

her children ate tomato sandwiches and stews

and she canned them for the winter

at seven o'clock the table was all green beans

from the neighboring farm

and peaches from the front yard

and there was space for everyone

and the tomatoes were honored,

and the children were happy,

and the farmer was filled to the brim with sunshine

and the sunshine loved every bit of this.

After

we eat shit

then we feel like shit

then we shit on each other

we live in shit and we drive shit cars

and then the shit cars shit on the earth

and then we treat each other like shit in our shit cars

that shit on the earth

while eating shit

and we look around our world and cry and say

wait what happened

because i hate to feel and it is all so much

and if we knew how far away we actually were

from true goodness

it would be a continent of hurt

When I Say Mental Disorder

I don't mean

Look at my meds

I don't mean

Read this book

I don't mean here is a pendulum

I don't mean padded walls

I don't mean try harder

I don't mean to speak for anyone else

I mean functioning is functioning

until the day you wake up

      and your heart is a broken boat

      I mean to say I am drowning in the enormity

      of my own missing pieces

I mean I can't move from this spot in the bed

I mean I can't put on a clean shirt

I mean I was only forming brain synapses when

my brain was opened and then closed

dad's devil

plucked the sutures like a harp

I cut holes in my own clothing

No one knew why I was an island

No one to stitch them up

I will wear all of these things with holes in them

Cut out like a map of only oceans

I don't know if I will name it joy

the brain does not work today

because the brain does not work today

because of the brain

because of the brain

because he

I Believe You (Sixteen)

I was sixteen and had a boyfriend that was an idiot

which was okay, I was also kind of an idiot

My friend and I snuck into an army barracks late at night

She was dating an older guy who lived on the base.

She slept in his room and I became a prize.

A building of a hundred men

drenched in America and sweat.

I'm not saying the military raped me—

I'm saying I was sixteen

and I was on my period.

I'm saying I was sixteen

and I didn't want to.

There were three wolves in the bedroom who circled me

without ever flashing their canines

(Isn't rape funny and tragic like that,

I have to speak in metaphor in order to get it out)

In the morning I told myself that I drank too much

and that I cheated, that I was so sorry

and boys will be boys

Weaved a different story in my head
Painted it like glitter in the swamp
Forced a laugh when I said
"rough sex"

I wonder how many girls have giggled
while they were raped.
I bet a lot of them.

Sometimes when I'm washing the dishes
the hairs on my arms stand up
thought memory turns physical memory
I don't know the science of that kind of thing
but I feel my eyes close scared
and the movie plays and I softly say
no and I don't
laugh uncomfortably this time

then afterward, the fury comes like a wave of ashes
and I pretend I am the biggest,
most powerful fucking phoenix
and as my hands wrap around the

coffee mug in the water

I pretend they teleport through time

and space to that night

and circle around his neck

and I say "no" a whole fuck ton louder than I did

I guess

what I'm saying is

I don't apologize like that anymore

Years I Have Forgotten

wow look

my left hand floats through my memory

and the particles lift

away—

like a bag of soccer balls, slowly

dumping out of a mesh bag into outer space

it is the most curious thing

my body

does not exist

from time to time

dad

what a terrible trick

Thoughts During Panic

flowerpots / crashing methodically / cartoon birds & big eyes / my optic

nerve / stuttering / you hate me / everyone hates me / a village

somewhere, hates me / I am swallowed / I am swallowing /

A memory horror / dirty hands / bad hands / greedy / the

coffin of my mind / and / gray matter / whispering /

short fires / mud of guilt / whispers again / kill

yourself / calm down / you are taking up /

too much space / overdramatic / making

it worse / drink something / but don't /

feed the demon / I will ruin the day /

I will ruin you / don't look at me /

shame / shame on me / hide /

find a dark / space / bury

myself in blankets / turn

off the lights / I will

sleep until you're

all dead / always

feel like a kid /

hear my mom

"she just

needs a

nap"

At 9:15 p.m. in a Small Bar in Pennsylvania

for Donald Trump

Trauma walks into a bar, orders a whiskey neat

All hungry-eyed boring holes through my dress,

I am numb and cannot turn away when he snaps

a dove neck in half, does not flinch.

All hungry-eyed boring holes through my dress,

I cannot shake the desire for literal murder, after all,

a dove neck in half does not flinch.

At 9:15 p.m., I begin the 23rd poem about my rape

I cannot shake the desire for literal murder, after all,

every woman has written this story:

At 9:15 p.m., I begin the 23rd poem about my rape.

I begin it with: Violation is a man with nice teeth

Every woman has written this story:

Trauma walks into a bar, orders a whiskey neat

Begin it with: Violation is a man with nice teeth,

snaps a dove neck in half, does not flinch

It Does Not End

Dear nineteen-year-old self,

I hear you whispering to that flashing black star.

yes, you are ugly in that nightgown.

you are ugly in that silver moon night,

crookedly holding a margarita.

you are as ugly as the day you were born.

as ugly as a field of tulips bursting red

as ugly as glittering snow on evergreens

as ugly as laughter.

mary, do you understand what I am saying?

you are a creation, a gift.

tell them you were born for this life.

tell them your heart is a bludgeoned castle,

tell them you've got room, you've got safe stone.

when they say that you laugh too much,

tell them that your laughter is a skeleton key.

you laugh because you've seen so much dying.

you laugh because living is an absurd joy.

to laugh is to be grateful for salt

for sweat, for crying. you know this.

mary, I know that the kitchen linoleum

feels like an answer to a puzzle.

I know you lay on it, chain-smoking, wishing

you were a supporting actor in someone else's life

or at the very least, a chipping floor.

something that stays in place; something not girl.

mary, stop trying to die.

I know sometimes you feel less than human

more like an unknown planet no one cares about

more like hot guilt

more like a catalog of trauma

mary, stop trying to die.

there is nothing better

than looking into the mirror

to discover infinite doors.

to witness your own bloom.

you are the best version of this story.

we're all waiting for you.

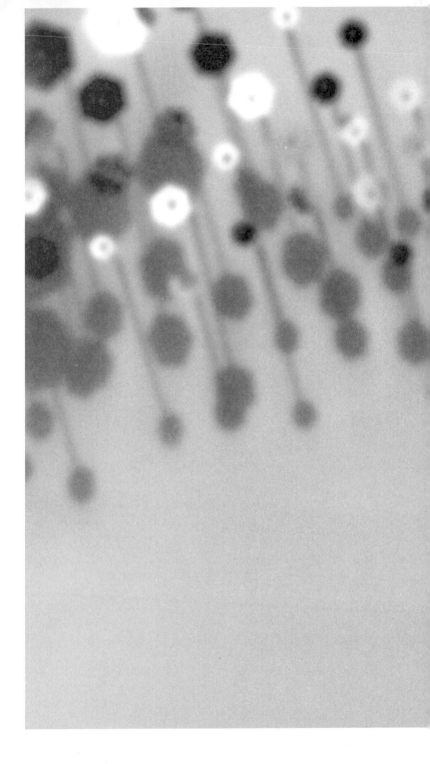

FOUR

Bless this whole shit show

Spring Is Here!

i didn't leave my bed today because
everything is so wonderful
just kidding i didn't leave my bed today
because i am depressed.
my friend Doc said *be ugly and love it*

i stay up until 7 a.m. watching porn and writing
emails to people i wish would love me back. i have
money everywhere but i don't collect it, it just sits in
"various accounts" & inner child me screams
about ice cream

inner child me screams about fish sticks and corn
dogs & why don't i have a boyfriend. inner
child me is also obsessed with death. Dear
blood, don't jump yet. Dear blood, I love you,
you are ugly, I love you.

Delicate Magic/Unhelpful Skills

I used to hear the word "love"

as in, "love will get you through

thirty years of marriage or

to the other side of IKEA"

but I thought it meant

whatever I need to be

to another person

whichever leg I need to hack

or habit forgotten,

I will kiss all your

empty cups

with bright lipstick, with a million

mattresses, with a spoonful

of teeth, will spill

over myself onto

myself for you

or, would you

rather me with blonde hair in the winter?

I can acrobat myself into you? is that love?

or is that just

some kind of space filled with space

like a

shadowkiss

or a dog holding its own leash or

a phantom tongue

stuck to a memory of winter

you asked me why I was crying once

while I was spiraling in shame

all I could get out was

I don't know how much of me

is just space for you

I Don't Think I've Ever Been So Lonely

I hate you. the burden of your leaving. I hate you so
much. I hate that you left that stupid couch. left me
to navigate the housefire scared and alone, you didn't
call me back. I forgot what your face looks like, you
know. I forgot the shape of your teeth. the wide grin
of joy I used to kiss.

I was a fucked-up bird. dead on the road trying to
be better every day. I thought I almost got there. I
thought I could be an angel. I lie next to the fireplace
alone now and I hate it. I hate your windowed eyes.
I hate the way you left. I hate the way you left the
house, you left it so pristine. I walked with you in
the woods, to the market, tried to match your pace.
I could never keep up. I was always the shit show,
a drunken morning. always trying to olympic pole
vault to meet you there—
I don't want you anymore.

You are dead to me, the cat is dead, I am a widow,

I am a windowless

room, a hazard to all, to you. an ache of forgetting,

a stupid whisper, the fervent beating of your ghost

heart in the hall, a vial of lavender, your things are

still here, my music is too loud. I smelled like a waste

to you, I was so unclean, so dangerous, running from

myself to get to you. look at this wreck, this mess,

the complete disaster that love makes, turns two

good people into one epitaph, god, I hope I forget

you soon.

Forensics

I have begun making a list of all the things you've
left unearthed for me to discover after you moved
out. you left while I was gone & you have not left
a note. you have not left a text or any otherworldly
space message that has been invented. There is no
psychic trill in between my ears, no email. I have
not been able to see you or hear you or touch you for
weeks, I only have little clues sprinkled around the
house like a torturous horror film. I am not laughing.
I am screaming at your couch in the basement. HOW
COULD YOU LEAVE ME. Do you hear me?? I
think that you are not that cruel. you left one book
for me in the kitchen with my name on it: a french
dictionary. this is the only handwritten thing left.

you left the incense, your key, the garage door
opener. you half made the bed—no sheet,
pillowcases off. shuffled the furniture around so your
stuff missing wouldn't be so glaringly obvious, took
paintings and hung other ones so the walls wouldn't

be bare. left one brown mug with turquoise inside
it because you know it was my favorite, you left the
bear jar because I drank out of it the day we met,
you left the slimy red pepper in the drawer because I
promised I'd take it out, you left the green powder in
the fridge for safety, you took all the butter knives,
left the games, took your good plates, left me the
flower ones, all the tea, you left me, I can't move, the
bed is so cold.

Nighttime Activities with a New Person

clutch. breath as hunger. closer. more.

electric palm, the Right spot

nails into your back. soft. hipkiss. a wish for more hands.

all of your mouths wrapped around all of my mouths

hard. guiding you, guiding me, little bites,

wild teeth, warm neck, pull, tremor, pull again

the part where your lips are a city

your lips are a city and I am a gasping wonder

your lips are a city and I am hushed

your lips are a city and I am a choir of yes

I am a choir of oh, fuck

of how do you know

how do you know how to do this thing to my body

my body, nails indented like crescent moons,

the pulpit of a greedy mouth

the sweat. my thighs. undone. held breath.

clutch again. eyes closed.

eyes open.

Margaritas

My first collection of poetry was titled,
500 Tips for Fat Girls
It was meant as a sarcastic jab to our thin-obsessed culture

If I had a do-over, I would call it
500 Tips for Being a Human

Because when the press asked about it—they said,
"So what ARE the tips?"
And sometimes I would laugh
and I would say "MARGARITAS"

but really I wanted to say

No, I don't have any advice
(aside from always put chips in your sandwich)

Honestly? Any advice about being fat is tragic
being fat should just mean that you get more awesome chairs!
that you get more hugs!

I watch TV shows with fat characters

Hoping for the story that never comes

The fat ladies are always apologizing for their size

They are never getting fucked

They are looking at donuts longingly

I want to watch the fat lady win

I want her to stop apologizing for being fat

I wish I could say: Hey, perfect angel cutie pie:

You don't owe anyone shit.

Stop apologizing for who you are.

Go eat a fucking sandwich and throw your scale away

Work out if you want to, lay on the couch if you want to

No one else lives in your body

You are enough, as you are, today.

God Damn You, Sarah McLachlan

sometimes when i cry, i start to cry harder
simply because i am crying or
i cry because i know that in the world somewhere there
are perfect little girls that are wearing fun tutus and
singing christmas songs or because there are actual
shar-pei puppies that look like rolled-up towels
or because on the internet you can find
pictures of pigs in rainboots

because sarah mclachlan comes onto my TV and sings to
animals who don't have homes and
i cry because they call me fat even though i am fat and
most of the time i don't care but some of the time i do care
because a word is just a word until it is not just a word,
it is a weapon.

i cry when there is no end and i cry because there is
an end and i cry because you love me so well and i cry
because i gave my love to other people before you and
i cry because i used to cry alone, because i wanted

to die, and then i cry harder because your shoulder
is so soft, i cry because the sunset is so beautiful
on the connecticut river, i cry because i am scared
i am losing my mind, i cry because i'm on meds, or
because i forgot my meds, or i'm crying for the fact
i'm crying because i forgot my meds and does this
mean i am actually myself, and i'm crying because i
am not actually myself, or i'm crying because maybe i
am myself and that doesn't feel like enough

i cry because i'm human and i'm connected and
there is immense sadness in the world. i cry because
humanity is frightening. because one person
consumed with self-hatred and armed with one gun
can kill an entire room of people. i cry because shame
propels so many of us. i cry because so many people
forget how important it is to cry, are made to feel
weak when they do. i cry because i want to close my
eyes to the world. i cry because i can't.

and i cry because there is also good. there is also
chocolate cake and love and harry potter and the
brilliant gasps of magic of holding a hand and also

hammocks! i love hammocks! there are also first
kisses and second kisses and love letters!

i cry because it is late in the summer, and all the fireflies
are winking at me and the moon is out and it wants
nothing from me.

i cry because i am full now and sure and say yes when
i mean yes and no when i mean no and can love you
with all of my breath, with all of my yes. i cry because i
stand on the cliff of humanity's magic, and i don't want
to jump anymore.

i cry because i am so well,
because i live so well
and how could one person
possibly be so fortunate
to live with all of this light

Today I Bought a Dream Journal
to Be Less Sad, Am Still Sad
but with Dream Journal

In the dream, I'm weak, standing on a lunch table,
hoarse and screaming repeatedly, "feel something!"
to an empty cafeteria

Have you tried apple cider vinegar or rhodiola or
lamotrigine or tomatoes from the garden

a slit opens up where I once cut myself and a flood
of white birds race, keep crashing into a mural of the
mascot, a whale, my heart

meditation apps or this book about mania or my friend is
a counselor or the ocean or crystals or you're not alone

tiny wings, rapid and panicked and hopeful, scream
from my wrists in between heaving sobs, turn into a
claylike powder at impact

—

a cabin in the woods or service animals my friend has a rat
even or call your sister in japan or light candles or write it out

no one is there and the birds keep coming and dying
and the house of dirt keeps growing along the wall,
I can't see the mural, it's my fault

watch videos of survivors or go for a walk or pilates or call
your friends back we miss you

the dirt looks like brown sugar now, is the size of my
sparkling grief, covers the whale, I don't even have
my palms open, giving up

journaling or steamed greens or tarot cards or have you tried
not wanting to die so much

Conversations with My Mother
in Places I've Lived

Backyard of the Yellow House, 1997

This isn't what love looks like.

I just want you to know that.

I know, Mom.

The Humphrey, on the phone, 2011

I cried for nine hours straight.

Will you please get back on medication?

I'll think about it.

South Everett, on the phone, 2007

I feel too much. I feel everything. I'm going crazy.

Why don't you come home? You don't look well.

She takes care of me. I take care of her too.

Dad's Third Eviction, 1995

The dog next door is trying to kill me, I think.

Your father is worse.

I know.

Katie's Couch, on the phone, 2010

You're drinking a lot, Mary.

I'm training for my birthday. Birthdays are like the drinking Olympics.

Stop trying to make me laugh.

Nassau House, 2009

I'm happy for you. The floors are wood, even.

And everyone gets their own room?

Yes, and a guest bedroom. For if you ever need any help.

Massachusetts, on the phone, 2016

But this is my home now. Why are you crying? I visit all the time!

You are so far away.

It Is Time to Eat Something Other Than Pizza and Tequila

After a mostly sedentary two weeks of intermittent crying and listening to Tori Amos, I have decided to venture out as a fragile sad queer among the nighttime college babes and go to the grocery store. It is time to stop crying.

At the four-way stop after the bike path on Maple, there are a few streets that connect the farms into town. Sorry if I'm not explaining it well, I've never done this by myself. She usually tells the directions part. There is a cucumber farm around there I think, something aromatic. I remember her liking the way that it smelled. I remember the night we had to pull over because the moon was so rich and orange and full of love. We stood holding hands in silence, being welcomely swallowed by the open night, the smell of cucumbers, the last twilight of summer still warm on our cheeks. As I drive by tonight, the road reminds me.

The stars start whispering,

    look up, look up.

It knocked the wind out of me. It was just the way

it happened—farm houses dotted with

Christmas lights, the air too cold to breathe now,

a sad Christmas song on the radio,

my chest caving in on itself

I pulled over just to see what it would feel like,

but the moon disappeared, I'm not lying

pulled from under my feet, the moon, it was you

you were there and then you were not

and this isn't a dream.

this is what dying feels like,

what it means to knife and be knifed

by the one that you loved

and to keep driving home anyway—

oh, my love, what have I done

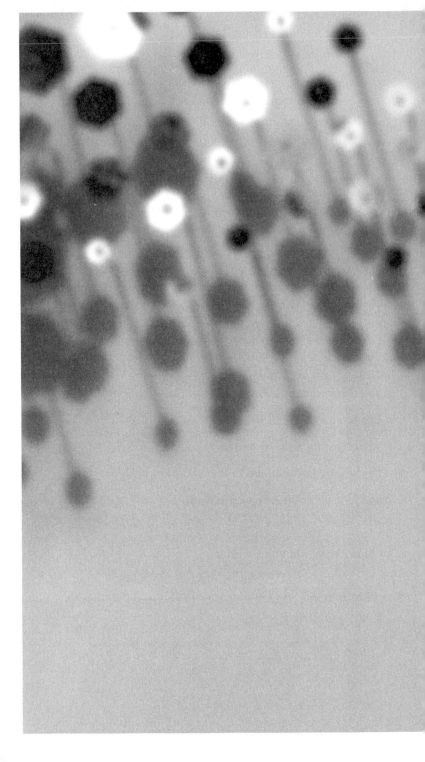

FIVE

Started from the bottom,

now I can pay my bar tab

June 2013, Singing at the Staples Center and Everyone Looks Hungry

My dad was a blue shell of a bad man. Mom talks
about his brain surgery, says it like this: "it changed
him," says it slowly, says it deliberately, nodding
her head to agree with herself. She is slow like this
because we both know what happens after. Clusters
of dirt in my hair, forgotten meals, the bright lights,
empty, empty, empty, and the pit. Shame is a pit.
Fills my name with a bunch of songs I don't know,
don't care to know, someday will wake up and sing
them out loud. It's not your fault, it's not your fault,
stupid white choruses of apology eyes over and over.
I say *stupid* in this way because my mom acts like I
remember. I don't remember anything. I'm crying in
the green room. My body isn't mine, it's my father's,
it's father's day. They're chanting my name in the
arena. Get it together. Ten thousand people tonight.

We both know what happens after. Bright lights,

empty, empty, empty, crying to my own pitless song.
Ten thousand people singing my stupid name, nod,
my body isn't mine. It's Father's Day.

Mom says slowly, deliberately: "Your body is an arena."

I am a blue meal of remembering. Ten thousand people
in the pit tonight, they're all bad fathers.

The Talk Show Host

I.

the question they most grin with crest-white teeth and
artificial inflection translates to: "aren't you so much
better than who you were before?"
I don't know, billy.
I feel the same. I feel love all the time.
I feel invaded sometimes.
I feel happy tears when I see people holding hands.
I am still many pages in a fucked-up book,
illustrating all the ways that trauma creates art
you know what. I feel powerful, billy. I feel seven years
old. I am doing okay. I am sad that I can't even keep a
plant alive and I miss my family. I love to sing and I love
to write and I love that it is my job, but it also complicates
passion for art when you depend on it for rent.
My friends are my employees and that feels weird, but
is also fun.
It is complicated.

—

I am so hungry for their tan-faced questions to
be genuine—
for eye contact on a red carpet instead of glancing at
the evening sheen of other more important people

> *Mary! How different is the world now*
> *that you're a star,*
> *not just a bartender anymore!*
> *right, sweetheart?*
> *does the sun*
> *glitter when you shit now,*
> *cupcake?*

During the week I performed at the 2014 Grammys, I
was promoting my single. An interviewer asked me on
live television, without warning or relevance, to talk
about my rape and how I overcame it. I will not tell
you what I said. I will tell you what I should have said.

II.

Billy, do you have a daughter

Does she smell like christmas morning

Do you laugh at the way she dances in her socks

in the kitchen

Do you sometimes cry knowing that her coming of age

is equal parts grieving and pride

When she gets excited, does she cyclone out of herself

like balloons in the wind

Is it beautiful

Are you proud like a gold bird

If someone hurt her, would you wish to decapitate them

slowly with hawklike precision and

burn their eyeballs out with acid

good

because that is what love is

In a parallel world, I am your daughter

Maybe at the kitchen table crying, you ask me

about the night I was raped

You hold honest eye contact,

not two strangers; vacant cells, oblivious

you take my hands like churches,

praying for another reality,

you let me tell you about the teeth

of the wolves at my thighs

You want to kill them with your bare hands

without a thought

you let me ruin your crisp TV shirt

with my sobbing

I want to rewrite everything bad

that ever happened to me

Billy, I don't know how this works

I've never had a dad

The Taking

Let this be called the Taking
Let it be called Gorgeous Art
Let it be called Bad Contract
Oh, friends, how bountiful your cups
are from all of the gifts you took
I watched you adorn your thievery
in articulated eloquence,
meticulously package it, calculated—
And then call it business
Yes, we should call this Business.
I say it again with hot tears on my cheeks—
Business.
Let this be called
Rich curtains that hang in a home
so extravagant I cannot even fathom
Forget all I said before—
Every Man For Himself
Every Man For Himself
Every Man

Every Man that ever Took from me

Could have called it business

Park Avenue

There is music sweating in the heels of Manhattan today

I mean to say Everything is sticking to Everything

Above ground, the clothes are clinging

to a woman holding her child's puckered hand

Frank Sinatra echoes from a storefront that sells

half-priced boots

When I take the train from New York,

the landscape undresses for us

We are voyeurs to her dance

See the neighborhoods that have swept

their ugly secrets

underneath the chevron rugs of new american restaurants

and cupcake shops

The high-rises on the east side don't know how

to hide the kids who cling to the gates further down

Park Avenue covering their ears when the train passes

It isn't always pretty, the train says,

but at least it's honest

the train is telling a story about power and money

who gets a piece of the pie

and who owns the pie factory

I don't even like pie,

but I keep buying pastries in heaps

because I can

I Wish Powerful Men Would Stop Being Fucking Terrible

I listen to Debussy because he moves me

the harmonic intricacies swell around mangled trees

thirsting for Spring

I wonder if Debussy was an asshole

or if he cried a lot

and what would his favorite cupcake be

and which BuzzFeed quiz would he take

and I wonder if he ever bought flowers for a lady

Or what he would choose for his cover photo

If he would have a hard time unfriending old

university colleagues who post annoying stuff like

"I ate a sandwich today. Pastrami! #blessed"

I wonder if Debussy would hate me because I like women

Do we love Picasso and Renoir and Schumann

the same way we loved Bill Cosby?

Would you love *Starry Night*

or Mozart's Requiem just the same

if you knew the artists beat their children or raped

their neighbor's daughter?

Can we separate art from the artist?

Is television an art form?

I don't know—

The internet has emptied a lot of secrets

of people who did not want them known, people

who were banking on the silence that shame makes

I wonder if my children will watch *The Cosby Show*

A Poem to Cheer You Up

When you think about it, there are a lot

of people that haven't died yet!

Think about it! How many dead people

have you met today?

You used to be one tiny microscopic insignificant thing,

swimming aimlessly in a nutsack

and out of all the other spermies,

you made it to that egg first!

Then, you survived childbirth! Can you imagine? Wow!

Then, you survived middle school!

A locker room! Somehow!

and now, you vibrant, stunning, living thing:

you get to love other people

and that love doesn't ever expire!

it is endlessly perfect!

Whenever I think that there might not be a god,

I think about that

Uber Driver #237

I came home crying to my girlfriend

she says *who did this to you*, and I say

My love, that man was a small gun

I say that you are a 27-year-old who never kissed anyone

I say you are a shard of glass I clutch tightly on purpose

A world I don't know

A suit of silence

I say you are sorry and that you didn't mean it

That you are a crocheted knife

Now tucked in the folds of my memory as a list of men

who took without asking

I say honestly

You are a driver I had at 2 a.m.

after I drank tequila with drag queens in

Colorado

And I wanted to be your friend

So when you forced my head to your mouth

with greedy hands

All I could think of was *how quickly I will forget this*

Because a man violating a woman is a boring story

A dumb horror film

how I recoiled and shook and lost speech

That I said loudly *you don't mean to do this*

you can't do this

I am not for you

instead at the shower tiles

Sometimes when I turn the stove on for tea

I don't remember even doing it

Of course, ten minutes later,

the shrill whistling startles me like a horror movie

And I am reminded of what actually is.

Glamorous Dressing Rooms Are Just Locker Rooms with Fake Plants

Over cocktails in the Fanciest Place I Have Ever Been,

he tells me sometimes he wishes the plane would crash

That the world does not look like what he thought it would

I say, me too.

I say, humans were not meant to live this way

I say, fame is a terrifying sword,

and I know how the luxury gleams in the light

and yes, you can sing with a blade in your side

Hit all of the right notes

and never let them know

Their eyes will marvel at your composure

But at some point,

the tide rises

you are snapping

And not in the teen angsty way of snapping

but in the way the slightest thing can undo you.

like how the weight of a feather is not much,

but it is everything when you are an insect

We spend our days in this macabre waltz

That because millions of people would break their legs to

stand on a stage like this

That it is somehow not okay to cry

Or say "I miss my family"

Or "today I hate my body"

Or to question "why me?"

You are the real *Truman Show*, friend

And everyone is watching tonight

I know all too well how to paint your face after crying

and the recitation of

"I'm so humbled" and "everything is surreal"

become part of a language that begins to feel disingenuous

Are you not the same boy

that cried in your room wanting friends?

Is this not what you wished for?

Are you not the same boy unfolding in front of millions?

Isn't that the crux of it all—

To be loved by all, and yet not believe it.

Dear friend,

May you walk out of a dark dressing room of fake plants,

May you never forget how the light looks at sunrise

How every day it is new

and how it wants nothing from you

Think of the birds on the tarmac

They congregate obliviously

like they might not ever die

May you claim your own path to what

makes you feel the most alive

The greatest thing about your life,

is that you're in it and you are awake

And you can do whatever you damn well please

I Don't Think It Was Milli Vanilli's Fault

1.

I am in a conference room
with nothing in it besides some money eyes,
an absurdly long conference table,
and swivel chairs that recline
My eyes glaze over the panorama of Los Angeles.
I am a product. I am not really here.

The next day, I am in "cool executive dude" room #3
Platinum albums hung up around the room, a low
brown leather couch, more sparkling plaques sit lazily
on the floor (Perhaps he is too busy to hang those ones
up. Maybe he has been installing solar panels in his
silver lake dude palace)

I am trying to remember the youtube video I saw
about power stances and awkwardly place my hands
behind my head and recline slowly, nearly
Falling backward. This does not feel

like a feminist move, it feels like a skit about what not to
do in a job interview put on by angsty high school kids.

I leave the meeting. I return a year later a different person
Maybe worse, I don't know.
I have more shoes than I did before.
I remember the feeling of all the snakes
fighting for the mouse
I remember all the nights I whispered to the moon on
all the red eye flights, asked her to pull me to space,
end this obnoxious ladder climbing,
this not-good-enough, this rocket to hell
I wish the car would crash
The year is a garbled phone call and it sounds like guilt

2.

don't squander this   don't

you want success   you really should

be so lucky to

cut off your arms   no one cares

if   you a c t u a l l y play piano   we've got

twenty pianists   focus on

you,   the star,   you've really

got something special   can I just sink my teeth into

your

musicblood   I hate to say this, but   Target

(We)   won't care/won't carry   your album   if

you   talk   about rape

in   the meantime   Here's a song by Sia

a song by Pink

a song by Colbie Caillat's guitarist   Can't you

just sing it   If you

do this ridiculous thing now   Jesus don't

be difficult   You can do what you love after

the after the after the after the after the   after

the   a f te r t h e

after the after

after the afte   r th e a f te r th e af t

er th e afte r   t h e af t e r t h e

a f te r t h e

after the   afte   r t h e   afte r th e

after after after after after after

after afrerafer t affert   affret after   afret a

fffffter   t   h   e

radio hit.

don't be ungrateful.

anyone would kill for this.

Blockbuster Hit!
A Girl Cries in Her Hotel Room!

[LOS ANGELES. IT IS MORNING. CHARACTER IS NOT BRAVE]

                    VOICE 1
        [calls from SL, crying to no one,
        is cyclone of herself]

                    VOICE 2
        nothing nothing nothing

                    VOICE 3
        the perpetual shame of every kiss,
        every cauterized song

                    ENSEMBLE
        your love does not exist

                    VOICE 4
        [over the shoulder]
        "not good"   a dress
        climbs out of her mouth

                    VOICE 5
        slut, [windowless room, curtains grating
        on themselves]

                    VOICE 6
        every pair of eyes, a dagger

                    VOICE 7
        every pair of eyes, a bathtub

                    VOICE 8
        [exit laughing, twirling in a gown]

                    ENSEMBLE
        how will you love like this

    [CHARACTER DOES NOT SLEEP, MELTS INTO THE CARPET,
    OFFERS EMERALDS TO NO ONE]

                    VOICE 9
        They're watching you [shaking, head
        tics up, head backward, alien self]

                    VOICE 10
        They're watching you as a black hole,
        hiding a dead girl

                    VOICE 11
        [to self] bury her on hyperion or in a
        park or in a dream

                    VOICE 12
        "thirty-one stories up"

    [CHARACTER'S ARM DETACHES, PLACES IT GENTLY
    ON THE STATIONERY]

                    VOICE 13
        crawls inside herself. So much
                                to forgive

    [LEAVES A TWENTY ON THE PILLOW.
    KISSES THE DOORFRAME, REMOVES LIPS]

VOICE 14

wash your hands of this [turns to
audience, vomiting diamonds] "I'm a
stupid woman, always swallowing myself
like this"

VOICE 15

[laughs sarcastically] your heart is
not a mirror

VOICE 16

[burns both hands, enters hell] your
heart is not a mirror

ENSEMBLE WEEPS

this love is not for you,

[CHARACTER IS PARALYZED IN SHEETS]

VOICE 17

she is knocking on the room next door

VOICE 18

[whispers to audience] is named Ella or
Gwendolyn or another kind of storied
princess, she just wants a window to
jump out of

VOICE 19

VOICE 20

[FADES TO BLACK, CRIMINALLY QUIET]

Dear YouTube Comments

Inspired by Lindy West

what would most make you happy?

what would most make you delight in your own skin?

Have you ever received flowers from anyone?

Ever?

Is it hard to be so knife-like?

My little sister told me that she buried

a flower once after accidentally picking it.

Can you imagine that kind of humanity?

Or do you find yourself ripping

the heads off daffodils and laughing?

Did someone once cut out your heart with

flippant hands and you forgot how to speak kindly?

When you fell, did they press their boot

against your chin and say

"Suck it up, pansy"

Did you stay that way for a while after that unkindness,

powerless

It hurts a lot less when you can't see

your own blood, doesn't it

when you close your eyes like a night shade,

you can pretend the blade in your side

is just a hiccup after pot roast

The mind is a mother like that

"kill yourself, you fat cow"

"you deserved to be raped"

oh daisy, oh lily, oh marigold

There are so many of us

"shut up hefer"

"girls like her make me sick"

Do you know how strange it is that any body

has an opinion on any other body?

Do you know that some people never find

what they love most about themselves?

That they spend their whole lives wishing

they were someone else?

Oh lilac, oh rosie

we are all flowers with our heads off

No one gave us a burial

"maybe you should sew your mouth shut"

Have you ever loved anyone so much,

that you wanted to bring them flowers

every

precious

morning?

P.S. u are a sad and depressin fuk, too

We Call These Creative Differences

Talked Friday / your career / the album / not trying /
to control / or upset you. But / frustrated / seriously /
detrimental to the process. / conflicting / your
management thinks / is the best way / successful
record. / major-label / the process / commercial
viability / Last record / achieved such little success /
entirely opposite / how you expressed you / wrong
place / formally / relieve you of your contract /
yourself. Additionally, / indifference toward success
/ or a hit. unwillingness / and / not commercially
successful / product / we have / artists / hit-makers. /
you are trying to avoid / "Success" to us / millions /
radio hits to follow / pop / ten times the amount / last
year / I would have felt / some reassurance. I respect
/ The bottom line / you seem to not / take advantage
/ expressed no desire / writing the album yourself /
not a path / none of us are comfortable / with you /
The truth is / you have not had a hit / you / desperately
need one. / financially / terrible /
commissions / frustrating / and your career / a

downward slope. The momentum / gone. No desire /
to take outside songs and you / caused this / every
mainstream booker / passed on / no shows / Because
the melancholic mood of your set / on the decline.
Star potential / no one really knows / "Same Love" /
three years ago. / We believe / will not yield /
Getting a hit that excites us / you refuse / co-writing
you want to be "unique" / major label
become / established / manager / extremely powerful
you cannot have / life. Not trying / blindside /
consider what I have said.

Thanks,

Foreign Feeling of Beauty

to Katie Pellegrino, Debora Spencer, Autumn de Wilde,
Shervin Lainez, Mindi Gilyeat Skidds,
and anyone who's ever fluffed my hair

Remember when you took your senior photos
And you felt like a model,
And how the photographer encouraged you
and occasionally murmured,
"stunning."
You understood how people could do that for a living
wear new clothes and hear "stunning" over and over again
"stunning"
and when you cried at how sublime
it was to be called stunning
and what a strange feeling that was
and how that foreign feeling of beauty
was kind of lonely, wasn't it?
That you never felt that way before? In your whole life?

looking at the spread of negatives on the kitchen table
you didn't want to ruin them with your small tears

Remember after the hair salon
When you stood in front of the mirror
in sheer disbelief while
Mindi fluffed your hair
this way and that
and how it was a little bit sad that someone
thumbing their fingers through your
hair felt like a halo,
felt wanted

are there people that exist that feel like that all the time?
or does everyone cry when they've been ugly for so long
and hear "stunning"
How do I say that when I am alone and
feel so very heavy

If I Were an Artist,
I Would Paint You Joyful

i would paint laughing and i would paint a song
but the art is contorted, even in my mind.

it isn't what i told the brush to do. hey canvas,
hey red slop. my wrist is ugly & uncomfortable

here you are in my room, here you are crying
here you are crying about my leaving

here i am ruthless and gentle and wrong
i smear an orange star over your mouth

you are crying onstage. if i hate myself
enough, i can call it kindness

no, no look! a sunflower instead
a meadow filled with babies

—

the babies are dressed as sunflowers!

what joy! do you hear the music?

i can hear you weeping into the microphone

i am not an artist. it isn't beautiful.

I scratch out the meadow with my fingernail.

each stroke, tiny evil truths.

Morning Blessing, May 19th.

for Paige

I.

how could I deserve
this goodness, this
morning, O
I wish it were a whale,
so I may see
love,
heaven. sweat. real
stupid, ridiculous
music in my body—
I only care
if it's you
at the end of the aisle/
the tourniquet
you you you you you
I am a ready and able
offering,
my love. I want the
ache & ghost and
kiss, this life with you.
synthesis of stars,
you, my forever heart,
the brilliantly obvious
angel calling to me
in the evening—
god I want to wake up
every morning,
and again after that.
Bless you

hands? to kiss all
unwavering beauty. O
—is it god? bless this.
bless it fiercely & blue
this moment of royal
this weight of
love, the infinite
love, this welcome
village
of dancing
& me
you carry the stars
on my charred heart
& me & us & lucky—
paradise
listen. time is a fool
now & then & forever
oh bless this
present ocean. holy
shameless love. Bless
the selves I was before
now. Bless that hell
again. that hell
is part of my history.
with you,
night & moon & kiss.
everything is so alive.
Bless you again

Acknowledgments

I would like to thank my editor, Kate Farrell, for being a champion of this book. I am grateful for your thoughtfulness and positivity and enthusiasm for such a depressing book of poems. I would also like to thank everyone at Macmillan, Henry Holt, and Feiwel & Friends for believing in my book and letting me be the unicorn queen of my manuscript. I feel so lucky to have a team this supportive of my voice and writing.

I would also like to thank Sara Brickman, who saved this book. Sara painstakingly line edited these poems and gave such thoughtful, brilliant critiques that have forever impacted my writing. So grateful for you and your spirit and your perfect laugh.

I would like to thank Marc Kaplan for inviting me to perform at his daughter's school fundraiser, where I read some poems, and was introduced to Kate from Henry Holt. Divinity is a good friend.
So are you, Marc.

I do not do any of this alone and have a team of wonderful people who deserve recognition for their support, energy, and vision. Thank you Nadia Schuessler, Simon Green and everyone at CAA, Alyssa Fasolino, Kat Eves, Gihan Salem, Brian Giggey, Amy Gravesande, Tim Mendonsa, Carole Kinzel, Shervin Lainez, and Micaela Lattanzio.

Thank you to my family: Mom, Anne, Hannah, Kat, Catie, Jer, Amy. As mom said once, *you are all wonderbeings with skin on*. Thanks for letting me be a true weirdo.

Thank you to everyone I have loved, kissed, crushed on, sent unsolicited love poems to. Thank you to everyone who has broken my heart. I don't know if that broken heart part made me a better person, but it did make me a better writer.

Paige, you are my favorite chapter of this story. I am the luckiest.

Tim, you are my friendship hotdog. Thank you for letting my cry at you for the last ten years. Thank you for keeping me alive on the nights I felt myself drowning in the enormity of shame.

Kristen, thank you for always being in my corner.

Nadia, I hope we get to laugh and drink wine on the porch until we die.

Julien, you are a gift to the world. I am grateful for your friendship.

Mal, thank you for seeing me when I felt so contorted by heartache. I hope to always know you.

Hollis and Rose, where would I be without you? Who would I be? Thank you.

Sara Ramirez, it is an honor to know you. Thanks for letting my cry on the phone at you. Here's to more nights of self-reflection, honesty, cocktails, and lamenting about the utter fuckery of love.

Cutrone, praise the divine goddess for you and your

grace, power, and wisdom. I'd happily start a fight in a restaurant for you any day if it means smashing the patriarchy with you and Ava.

Thank you to Youth Speaks, Brave New Voices, Winter Tangerine, Arts Corps, and The Seattle Poetry Slam.

This would be the dumbest page of acknowledgments if I didn't mention the poets I love, the poets that are friends, the poets that make me weep, the poets that have encouraged me to grow. There's a lot of them. Look every single one of them up. Buy their work: Shira Erlichman, Tara Hardy, Angel Nafis, Ebo Barton, Safia Elhillo, Brian Ellis, Rose McAleese, Rachel McKibbens, Rudy Francisco, Lauren Zuniga, Jon Sands, Buddy Wakefield, Anis Mojgani, Ada Limon, Aracelis Girmay, Morgan Parker, Hera Lindsay Bird, Ashley Lumpkin, Jesse Parent, Megan Falley, Richard Siken, Danez Smith, Franny Choi, Camonghne Felix, Nikkita Oliver, Maddy Clifford, Hollis Wong-Wear, Rachel Wiley, Chris Zweigle, Olivia Gatwood, Kim Selling, Jayy Dodd, Nina

Powles, William Nu'utupu Giles, Jamaica Osorio,
Muggs Fogarty, Denice Frohman, Doc Luben, Sarah
Maria Medina, Sierra DeMulder, Andrea Gibson, Sarah
Kay, Melissa Lozada-Oliva, Janae Johnson, Amber
Tamblyn, Brit Shostak, Roma Raye, Lana Ward,
Donte Johnson, Casey Tonnelly, Matt Blesse, Ken
Arkind, Mindy Nettifee, Denise Jolly, Amy Everhart,
Alaka'i Kotrys, Jovan Mays, Robyn Bateman, Imani
Sims, Robert Lashley, Shaun August, Clare Elliot,
Beau Sia, Jodie Knowles, Austin Mansell, Christian
Drake, Justice Ameer Gaines, Mike McGee, Roberto
Carlos Ascalon, Gibson Collins, Robin Park, Erich
Haygun, Jocelyn Ng, George Watsky, Matt Gano,
Danny Sherrard, Brianna Albers, Samantha Peterson,
El Dia, Ittai Wong, Elaina Ellis, Chrysanthemum
Tran, Stephen Meads, Eirean Bradley, Mud Howard,
Karen Finneyfrock, Sam Sax, Miles Walser, Hieu Minh
Nguyen, Elizabeth Acevedo, Joshua Jennifer Espinoza,
Tu Anh Phan, Jae Carroll, Chris Carroll, Joy Harjo,
Jeanann Verlee, Lucille Clifton, Aziza Barnes, Teresa
Siagatonu, Eve Ewing, Caroline Harvey, Simone
Beaubien, Mahogany L. Browne, Amber Flame, Troy
Osaki, Sean Patrick Mulroy, Yasmin Belkhyr, Natasha

T. Miller, Kirya Traber, Aaron Samuels, George Yamazawa, Jamila Woods, Porsha Olayiwola, Lydia Havens, Hanif Abdurraqib, Dominique Christina, Dåkot-ta Alcantara-Camacho, Jasmine Mans, Ronnie Rain, Ashlee Haze, Kaveh Akbar, Emily Rose, Patricia Lockwood, and Jack McCarthy, who beat me in my very first slam.